Abraham Lincoln

★ ★ ★ ★ ★ ★

by David Neufeld

Orlando   Boston   Dallas   Chicago   San Diego

Visit *The Learning Site!*

www.harcourtschool.com

Abraham Lincoln was the sixteenth president of the United States. He had the hard job of keeping our country together.

Abraham Lincoln was born in a tiny cabin on a farm in Kentucky. His family moved to Indiana when he was seven. When they got there, he helped his father build a log cabin.

His mother taught him to read and write. She also taught him to care for other people. She tried to help him go to school. He couldn't go to school very often.

Abe loved to read. He read the Bible and he read newspapers. He read everything he could find. He also loved to talk and to listen.

Abe loved to write. He wrote poems. He wrote about what was happening in Indiana. He wrote about the United States of America. He even wrote jokes.

There was hard work to do on the
farm. Abe plowed the land and
chopped wood. He grew strong
splitting trees into rails for fences. He
also grew very, very tall.

When he was twenty-one, Abe
moved to Illinois. He worked hard at
many jobs. He guided a flat boat down
the river. He saved his money and
bought a grocery store.

Abe made a lot of friends. People said he never lied. They liked to listen to him. He read more books and became a lawyer. Abe wanted to help people in trouble.

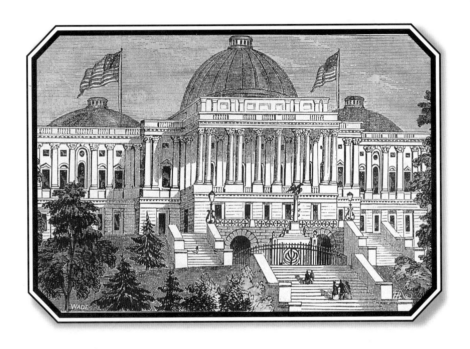

Our country's government was in
Washington, D.C. Abe wanted to go
there to help make the laws. He
decided to run for office and he won!

When Abraham Lincoln moved to
Washington, Americans had many
differences. People in the South used
slaves to work on farms. People in the
North did not think this was fair.

Abraham Lincoln spoke out about freedom for everyone. People cheered when he said that doing the right thing makes us strong. In 1860, Abraham Lincoln ran for president. He won the election.

Some people were unhappy that Abraham Lincoln won. Soon the country was at war. Eleven states chose to leave the United States and become a new country.

The armies of the North and South
fought. President Lincoln said the
United States must stay together. He
gave speeches about the heroes of
the war.

The war went on for four years. Many, many people died. President Lincoln worried about what was happening to the country.

Finally the war ended in 1865.
President Lincoln was so tired. He had
kept the country together. He was a
brave American hero.